MINI INSTANT POT COOKBOOK

SUPERFAST 3-QUART MODELS ELECTRIC PRESSURE COOKER RECIPES – COOKING HEALTHY, MOST DELICIOUS & EASY MEALS

BY PHILIP JOHNSON

CONTENTS

INTRODUCTION

With so many things to manage in one day, we are always surrounded by hundreds of small tasks to complete. Hectic life is no more a phase as it has been taken a permanent place in our fast-paced lifestyle. Time is always critical, be it for allotting for exercise, leisure, work or cooking. We are always constantly trying to save time so that we can spend more quality to with our family and loved ones.

Instant Pot is designed to cook meals in real quick time and without compromising its nutritional values. Instant Pot models come in various sizes, and the smallest one is of 3-quart; it is designed to make meals in smaller quantity for 2-4 servings and suits perfectly to make meals for 2-4 people. Instant Pot is a valuable investment as it does all the cooking functions by itself and saves you from spending long hours in the kitchen.

In this dedicated 3-Quart Instant Pot cookbook, you will find a hand-picked collection of Instant Pot recipes to prepare in a 3-Quart model at the comfort of your home. Making small size meals in Instant Pot is very easy and quick as it needs less amount of ingredients.

It suits perfectly for a small size family or couples. And with versatile cooking functions available, you can cook meals for various requirements including breakfasts, soups, stews, curries, appetizers, snacks, main course meals (chicken, meat, seafood, and vegetarian), and desserts.

Get ready to explore a vibrant collection of healthy 3-quart Instant Pot recipes for all your cooking needs. Let's get started.

Chapter 1: Instant Pot at A Glance

Instant Pot is a versatile cooking appliance that you can use to prepare all types of meals for everyday cooking needs. It uses high pressure steam to cook added ingredients, and its smart lock technology preserves nutrients by preventing them to be washed away. High-temperature steam enables food to cook in a matter of minutes, and thus it saves your precious cooking time.

MINI INSTANT POT (3-Quart)

The stylish MINI Instant Pot model is offered in the market with 3-quart cooking capacity.

This small model is offered in all three categories of ULTRA, DUO, and DUO PLUS.

Smart Features:

- It offers multiple programmable features (mentioned below in the book) with multiuse pressure cooking options (slow cooking, yogurt maker, pressure cooking, rice cooker, etc.

- Build using modern generation technology with easily programmable settings.

- It comes with a digital LED display and shows cooking time status.

- You can delay cooking time up to 24 hours.

- Automatic keep warm function that keeps cooked food warm for up to 10 hours.

- Fast and flexible cooking with 70% energy efficient models.

- Exterior is made from high quality durable stainless steel, and it is dishwasher safe.

Simple and Effective

In just a few steps, you can use Instant Pot for making all types of meals.

1. Take Instant Pot and open its top lid. Plug it on by stating the power switch.
2. Add the recipe ingredients in the cooking pot area. Gently stir them.
3. Close the lid, and now you have to select cooking function from various available choices.
4. Then after, you can set cooking time as per recipe ingredients.
5. Now, Instant Pot will start building pressure to cook added ingredients.
6. Just open the lid, after cooking time gets over.
7. Enjoy the recipe. It's as simple as it seems without any hassle.

DIFFERENT MINI INSTANT POT COOKING SETTINGS

Keep Warm/Cancel

With this cooking function, you can easily cancel the current cooking program that has been set by you previously. After pressing it, it sets Instant Pot in a standby mode and keeps inside recipe warm.

Manual

With this setting, you can manually set your pressure mode "HIGH" or "LOW" and cook time. You can also switch between the modes. The default mode is "HIGH" and used most commonly in cooking most recipes.

Rice

With this function, your Instant Pot converts into a rice cooker. It allows you to prepare various rice based meals and other cuisines easily. The default for this setting is automatic and cooks rice at low pressure. You can use "Adjust" setting to set your preferred time.

Slow Cook

With this function, your Instant pot converts into a rice cooker, which can cook to up to 40 hours. This function's default cooking time is 4 hours.

Poultry

With this setting, you can easily prepare all meals with chicken and poultry. This function's default cooking time is 15 minutes.

Bean/Chili

With this setting, you can easily prepare all types of chili or beans. This function's default cooking time is 30 minutes.

Multigrain

With this setting, you can easily prepare a mixture of grains such as brown rice, beans, wild rice etc. This function's default cooking time is 40 minutes of high pressure.

Cake & Egg

This setting is for a variety of cake and egg-based recipes.

Porridge

With this setting, you can easily prepare oatmeal or porridge of various grains. This function's default cooking time is high pressure for 20 minutes.

Meat/Stew

With this setting, you can easily prepare meats or stew. This function's default cooking time is 35 minutes.

Soup

With this setting, you can easily prepare a variety of broths and soups. This function's default cooking time is 30 minutes of high pressure.

Yogurt

This function's default cooking time is 8 hours of cooking time to make various types of yogurts. You can use "Adjust" to increase or decrease time.

Sauté

This setting is for sautéing ingredient without closing the top lid. This function is for browning, sautéing or simmering purpose.

Steam

You can use this function for steaming seafood, veggies or reheating foods. This function's default cooking time is 10 minutes of high pressure cooking.

COOKING FUNCTION TERMINOLOGY

NPR (Natural Pressure Release)

This setting means that you can set Instant Pot for naturally releasing inside pressure. Leave the vent valve alone until it comes down by its own after releasing all build up pressure.

QPR (Quick Pressure Release)

This means that you can set Instant Pot for quickly releasing inside pressure. It releases pressure in quicker was as compared to the above function.

THE INSTANT POT ADVANTAGES

Wholesome Food & Nutrition

Pressure cooking at high temperature ensures that heat is evenly distributed, when the cooking process is on.

The added ingredients are not necessarily required to be immersed in water; it simply requires sufficient water to immerse them. The vitamins and minerals save from being dissolved or leached away by water. You get to enjoy the wholesome food every day for your whole family.

Saves Time & Energy

MINI Instant Pot cook food much faster than any other traditional methods of cooking. By faster cooking, it saves up to 70% of energy that is used in other methods of cooking. Moreover, by cooking food at extremely high temperature, it cooks food in quick time and saves valuable cooking time.

Cooking Convenience

With multiple cooking options for various meals, you have a few buttons to push to start cooking and thus, offers you the ultimate cooking convenience. It offers more than 12 key-cooking functions. Moreover, it is easy to clean after cooking and thus, don't create any hassle while cleaning it.

Kills Micro-Organism

As mentioned before, MINI Instant Pot cook food at extreme high temperature and thus, it kills most of the harmful fungus, bacteria and other micro-organisms. It provides you with a completely safe and clean meals for your optimum fitness and wellness.

Cheddar Bacon Potato

Prep Time: 8-10 min.

Cooking Time: 7 min.

Number of Servings: 2

Ingredients:

- 1/2 teaspoon garlic powder
- 1 1/2 ounces cheddar cheese, grated
- 1 ounces ranch dressing
- 1 teaspoon parsley, dried
- 1/2 pound red potatoes, make medium size cubes
- 1 bacon strip, chopped
- A pinch of pepper and salt
- 1 tablespoon water

Directions:

1. Take your 3-Quart Instant Pot; open the top lid. Plug it and turn it on.
2. In the cooking pot area, add the bacon, parsley, salt, potatoes, pepper, garlic powder, and water. Using a spatula, stir the ingredients.
3. Close the top lid and seal its valve.
4. Press "MANUAL" setting. Adjust cooking time to 7 minutes.
5. Allow the recipe to cook for the set cooking time.
6. After the set cooking time ends, press "CANCEL" and then press "QPR (Quick Pressure Release)".
7. Instant Pot will quickly release the pressure.
8. Open the top lid, add the cooked recipe mix in serving plates. Mix in the cheese and dressing.
9. Serve and enjoy!

Nutritional Values (Per Serving):

Calories - 296

Fat – 9.5g

Carbohydrates – 41g

Fiber – 5.5g

Protein – 13g

Broccoli Egg Morning

Prep Time: 5-8 min.

Cooking Time: 5 min.

Number of Servings: 2

Ingredients:

- 3 eggs, whisked
- ½ cup broccoli florets
- A pinch garlic powder
- 2 tablespoons tomatoes
- 1 clove garlic, minced
- ½ small yellow onion, chopped
- ½ red bell pepper, chopped
- 2 tablespoons cheese, grated
- A pinch chili powder
- 2 tablespoons onions
- 2 tablespoons parsley
- Pepper and salt as needed

Directions:

1. Take your 3-Quart Instant Pot; open the top lid. Plug it and turn it on.
2. Open the top lid; grease inside cooking surface using a cooking spray.
3. In a bowl, whisk the eggs.
4. Add the remaining ingredients except the cheese. Season with Pepper and salt.
5. In the cooking pot area, add the mixture.
6. Close the top lid and seal its valve.
7. Press "STEAM" setting. Adjust cooking time to 5 minutes.
8. Allow the recipe to cook for the set cooking time.
9. After the set cooking time ends, press "CANCEL" and then press "QPR (Quick Pressure Release)".
10. Instant Pot will quickly release the pressure.
11. Open the top lid, add the cooked recipe mix in serving plates. Top with the cheese.
12. Serve and enjoy!

Nutritional Values (Per Serving):

Calories - 376

Fat – 28g

Carbohydrates – 9g

Fiber – 3.5g

Protein – 23g

Classic Buckwheat Porridge

Prep Time: 8-10 min.

Cooking Time: 6 min.

Number of Servings: 2-3

Ingredients:

- 1/2 teaspoon vanilla extract
- 1 banana, peeled and sliced
- 1/4 cup raisins
- 3 cup rice milk
- 1 cup buckwheat groats, rinsed

Directions:

1. Take your 3-Quart Instant Pot; open the top lid. Plug it and turn it on.
2. In the cooking pot area, add the raisins, milk, buckwheat banana, and vanilla. Using a spatula, stir the ingredients.
3. Close the top lid and seal its valve.
4. Press "MANUAL" setting. Adjust cooking time to 6 minutes.
5. Allow the recipe to cook for the set cooking time.
6. After the set cooking time ends, press "CANCEL" and then press "QPR (Quick Pressure Release)".
7. Instant Pot will quickly release the pressure.
8. Open the top lid, add the cooked recipe mix in serving plates.
9. Serve and enjoy!

Nutritional Values (Per Serving):

Calories - 386

Fat – 4g

Carbohydrates – 34g

Fiber – 7g

Protein – 8.5g

Classic Hash Brown Frittata

Prep Time: 8-10 min.

Cooking Time: 20 min.

Number of Servings: 2

Ingredients:

- 3 eggs
- 2 ounces hash browns
- 1/2 tablespoon butter, melted
- 2 tablespoons milk
- 2 tablespoons scallions, chopped
- A pinch of pepper and salt
- 1 small garlic clove, minced
- 2 ounces cheddar cheese, grated
- 1/2 teaspoon tomato paste
- 1 1/2 cup water

Directions:

1. In a bowl, mix the milk and tomato paste.
2. In another bowl, mix the eggs, garlic, scallions, salt, pepper and milk mix; combine everything.
3. Spread the browns into a greased baking dish; add the butter and pour eggs mix all over. Top with cheese.
4. Take your 3-Quart Instant Pot; open the top lid. Plug it and turn it on.
5. Pour the water and place steamer basket/trivet inside the pot; arrange the dish over the basket/trivet.
6. Press "MANUAL" setting. Adjust cooking time to 22 minutes.
7. Allow the recipe to cook for the set cooking time.
8. After the set cooking time ends, press "CANCEL" and then press "QPR (Quick Pressure Release)".
9. Instant Pot will quickly release the pressure.
10. Open the top lid, add the cooked recipe mix in serving plates.
11. Serve and enjoy!

Nutritional Values (Per Serving):

Calories – 346

Fat – 23.5g

Carbohydrates – 13g

Fiber – 2.5g

Protein – 18g

Yogurt Oats Morning

Prep Time: 5 min.

Cooking Time: 6 min.

Number of Servings: 2

Ingredients:

- 2/3 cup Greek yogurt
- 2/3 cup blueberries
- 2 tablespoons chia seeds
- 2/3 cup almond milk
- 2/3 cup old-fashioned oats
- 1/2 teaspoon vanilla
- 1 1/2 cup water
- 1 teaspoon sugar
- A pinch of cinnamon powder

Directions:

1. In a heatproof bowl, mix the milk, yogurt, blueberries, oats, chia seeds, sugar, cinnamon, and vanilla.
2. Take your 3-Quart Instant Pot; open the top lid. Plug it and turn it on.
3. Pour the water and place steamer basket/trivet inside the pot; arrange the bowl over the basket/trivet.
4. Close the top lid and seal its valve.
5. Press "MANUAL" setting. Adjust cooking time to 6 minutes.
6. Allow the recipe to cook for the set cooking time.
7. After the set cooking time ends, press "CANCEL" and then press "QPR (Quick Pressure Release)".
8. Instant Pot will quickly release the pressure.
9. Open the top lid, add the cooked recipe mix in serving plates.
10. Serve and enjoy!

Nutritional Values (Per Serving):

Calories - 239

Fat – 6.5g

Carbohydrates – 38g

Fiber – 10g

Protein – 8g

Berry Quinoa Morning

Prep Time: 5-8 min.

Cooking Time: 11 min.

Number of Servings: 2

Ingredients:

- 2 cups water
- A pinch of cinnamon powder
- 1 tablespoon maple syrup
- 1 cup quinoa
- 1/4 cup berries of your choice
- 1/4 teaspoon vanilla extract

Directions:

1. Take your 3-Quart Instant Pot; open the top lid. Plug it and turn it on.
2. In the cooking pot area, add the cinnamon, vanilla, quinoa, water and maple syrup. Using a spatula, stir the ingredients.
3. Close the top lid and seal its valve.
4. Press "MANUAL" setting. Adjust cooking time to 1 minutes.
5. Allow the recipe to cook for the set cooking time.
6. After the set cooking time ends, press "CANCEL" and then press "QPR (Quick Pressure Release)".
7. Instant Pot will quickly release the pressure.
8. Open the top lid, fluff the mix and add the cooked recipe mix in serving plates. Top with the berries.
9. Serve and enjoy!

Nutritional Values (Per Serving):

Calories - 354

Fat – 5.5g

Carbohydrates – 36g

Fiber – 6g

Protein – 11.5g

Tomato Beef Meatballs

Prep Time: 10-15 min.

Cooking Time: 20-25 min.

Number of Servings: 2-3

Ingredients:

- 1/2 yellow onion, chopped
- 1/2 pound beef, ground
- 1 garlic clove, crushed or minced
- 7 ounces tomato sauce
- 1 tablespoon olive oil
- 4 tablespoons rice
- A pinch of pepper and salt
- 1/2 cup water
- 1/2 tablespoon Worcestershire sauce

Directions:

1. Take your 3-Quart Instant Pot; open the top lid. Plug it and turn it on.
2. Press "SAUTÉ" setting and the pot will start heating up.
3. In the cooking pot area, add the oil, half of the garlic and onions. Cook until starts becoming translucent and softened for 3-4 minutes. Stir in between.
4. Add the water, Worcestershire sauce and tomato sauce, stir and bring to a simmer.
5. In a bowl, mix the rice, beef, salt, pepper, remaining garlic and onion.
6. Shape meatballs, and gently flatten them.
7. In the cooking pot area, add the meatballs.
8. Close the top lid and seal its valve.
9. Press "MANUAL" setting. Adjust cooking time to 15 minutes.
10. Allow the recipe to cook for the set cooking time.
11. After the set cooking time ends, press "CANCEL" and then press "QPR (Quick Pressure Release)".
12. Instant Pot will quickly release the pressure.

13. Open the top lid, add the cooked recipe mix in serving plates.
14. Serve and enjoy!

Nutritional Values (Per Serving):

Calories – 323

Fat – 17.5g

Carbohydrates – 24g

Fiber – 3.5g

Protein – 24g

Orange Brussels Sprouts

Prep Time: 5 min.

Cooking Time: 4 min.

Number of Servings: 2-3

Ingredients:

- 1 teaspoon orange zest
- 1 ½ teaspoon maple syrup
- 1 tablespoons butter
- ½ pound Brussels sprouts, trimmed
- A pinch of pepper and salt
- 3 tablespoons orange juice

Directions:

1. Take your 3-Quart Instant Pot; open the top lid. Plug it and turn it on.
2. In the cooking pot area, add the ingredients. Using a spatula, stir the ingredients.
3. Close the top lid and seal its valve.
4. Press "MANUAL" setting. Adjust cooking time to 4 minutes.
5. Allow the recipe to cook for the set cooking time.
6. After the set cooking time ends, press "CANCEL" and then press "QPR (Quick Pressure Release)".
7. Instant Pot will quickly release the pressure.
8. Open the top lid, add the cooked recipe mix in serving plates.
9. Serve and enjoy!

Nutritional Values (Per Serving):

Calories - 72

Fat – 3.5g

Carbohydrates – 6g

Fiber – 2g

Protein – 3g

Spiced Clam Appetizer

Prep Time: 10 min.

Cooking Time: 5 min.

Number of Servings: 3-4

Ingredients:

- 1/2 teaspoon oregano, chopped
- 1/2 cup breadcrumbs
- 1 cup water
- 2 tablespoons parsley, chopped
- 2 tablespoons parmesan cheese, grated
- 12 clams, opened and washed
- 1 garlic clove, crushed or minced
- 2 tablespoons butter

Directions:

1. In a bowl, mix the breadcrumbs, parmesan, oregano, parsley, butter and garlic.
2. Add the mix into the clams.
3. Take your 3-Quart Instant Pot; open the top lid. Plug it and turn it on.
4. Pour the water and place steamer basket/trivet inside the pot; arrange the clams over the basket/trivet.
5. Close the top lid and seal its valve.
6. Press "MANUAL" setting. Adjust cooking time to 5 minutes.
7. Allow the recipe to cook for the set cooking time.
8. After the set cooking time ends, press "CANCEL" and then press "QPR (Quick Pressure Release)".
9. Instant Pot will quickly release the pressure.
10. Open the top lid, add the cooked recipe mix in serving plates.
11. Serve with some lemon wedges and enjoy!

Nutritional Values (Per Serving):

Calories – 326

Fat – 26.5g

Carbohydrates – 28g

Fiber – 1g

Protein – 12g

Jalapeno Peanut Snack

Prep Time: 8-10 min.

Cooking Time: 60 min.

Number of Servings: 2-3

Ingredients:

- 1 small jalapeno, chopped
- 1/2 pound raw peanuts
- 1/2 tablespoon Cajun seasoning
- 2 garlic cloves, minced
- 2 tablespoons salt

Directions:

1. Take your 3-Quart Instant Pot; open the top lid. Plug it and turn it on.
2. Add the water, salt and peanuts; place steamer basket/trivet inside the pot.
3. Close the top lid and seal its valve.
4. Press "MANUAL" setting. Adjust cooking time to 8 minutes.
5. Allow the recipe to cook for the set cooking time.
6. After the set cooking time ends, press "CANCEL" and then press "QPR (Quick Pressure Release)".
7. Instant Pot will quickly release the pressure.
8. Open the top lid, add the cooked recipe mix in a bowl.
9. Mix in the Cajun seasoning, jalapeno and garlic; toss and serve.

Nutritional Values (Per Serving):

Calories – 458

Fat – 36g

Carbohydrates – 21g

Fiber – 11g

Protein – 21.5g

Fruity Raisin Salsa

Prep Time: 10 min.

Cooking Time: 18 min.

Number of Servings: 2

Ingredients:

- 1 small red hot chili pepper, minced
- 1/2 shallot, chopped
- 2 teaspoons ginger, grated
- 1 small apple, peeled, cored and chopped
- A pinch of cardamom
- 2 teaspoons olive oil
- A pinch of cinnamon powder
- 2 tablespoons white vinegar
- 2 tablespoons chicken broth
- 1 mango, peeled and chopped
- A pinch of salt
- 1 tablespoon raisins

Directions:

1. Take your 3-Quart Instant Pot; open the top lid. Plug it and turn it on.
2. Press "SAUTÉ" setting and the pot will start heating up.
3. In the cooking pot area, add the oil, shallot, ginger, cinnamon, chili peppers and cardamom. Cook until starts becoming translucent and softened for 3 minutes. Stir in between.
4. Add the mango, apple, salt, raisins, sugar and vinegar, chicken broth; gently stir.
5. Close the top lid and seal its valve.
6. Press "MANUAL" setting. Adjust cooking time to 15 minutes.
7. Allow the recipe to cook for the set cooking time.
8. After the set cooking time ends, press "CANCEL" and then press "QPR (Quick Pressure Release)".
9. Instant Pot will quickly release the pressure.
10. Open the top lid, add the cooked recipe mix in serving plates.
11. Serve with some crackers and enjoy!

Nutritional Values (Per Serving):

Calories – 255

Fat – 6g

Carbohydrates – 42.5g

Fiber – 9g

Protein – 3.5g

Oregano Pasta Chicken

Prep Time: 8-10 min.

Cooking Time: 12 min.

Number of Servings: 2

Ingredients:

- ½ teaspoon olive oil
- ½ cup diced tomatoes
- ¼ teaspoon salt
- 1 bay leaf
- 2 tablespoons chopped parsley
- ½ teaspoon pepper
- ½ cup chopped onion
- 1 ½ cup diced chicken
- ½ cup diced red bell pepper
- ½ teaspoon oregano

Directions:

1. Take your 3-Quart Instant Pot; open the top lid. Plug it and turn it on.
2. Press "SAUTÉ" setting and the pot will start heating up.
3. In the cooking pot area, add the oil and onions. Cook until starts becoming translucent and softened. Stir in between.
4. Add the diced chicken, bell pepper and tomatoes. Season with salt, pepper, oregano, and bay leaf then stir well.
5. Close the top lid and seal its valve.
6. Press "MANUAL" setting. Adjust cooking time to 10 minutes.
7. Allow the recipe to cook for the set cooking time.
8. After the set cooking time ends, press "CANCEL" and then press "NPR (Natural Pressure Release)".
9. Instant Pot will slowly and naturally release the pressure.
10. Open the top lid, add the cooked recipe mix in serving plates.
11. Serve with some pasta and parsley on top and enjoy!

Nutritional Values (Per Serving):

Calories - 123

Fat – 3g

Carbohydrates – 4.5g

Fiber – 1g

Protein – 16g

Chicken Soy Tortilla

Prep Time: 8-10 min.

Cooking Time: 10 min.

Number of Servings: 2

Ingredients:

- 1/2 pound chicken, ground
- 2 tablespoons soy sauce
- 2 teaspoons garlic, minced
- A pinch of ginger, grated
- 2 tortillas for serving
- 1 small yellow onion, chopped
- 2 tablespoons chicken stock
- 2 tablespoons balsamic vinegar
- A pinch of allspice, ground
- 4 tablespoons water chestnuts

Directions:

1. Take your 3-Quart Instant Pot; open the top lid. Plug it and turn it on.
2. In the cooking pot area, add the onion, garlic, ginger, allspice, chicken, chestnuts, soy sauce, stock, and vinegar. Using a spatula, stir the ingredients.
3. Close the top lid and seal its valve.
4. Press "MANUAL" setting. Adjust cooking time to 10 minutes.
5. Allow the recipe to cook for the set cooking time.
6. After the set cooking time ends, press "CANCEL" and then press "QPR (Quick Pressure Release)".
7. Instant Pot will quickly release the pressure.
8. Open the top lid, add the cooked recipe mix in serving plates.
9. Fill the tortillas, make wraps and enjoy!

Nutritional Values (Per Serving):

Calories – 310

Fat – 11g

Carbohydrates – 23.5g

Fiber – 1g

Protein – 23.5g

Nut & Date Chicken

Prep Time: 10 min.

Cooking Time: 30 min.

Number of Servings: 2

Ingredients:

- 1 teaspoon coriander, ground
- 4 chicken thighs, skinless and boneless
- A pinch of pepper and salt
- 1 teaspoon cumin, ground
- 1 teaspoon smoked paprika
- 1/2 tablespoon olive oil
- 1 garlic clove, crushed or minced
- Chopped mint for serving
- 1/2 yellow onion, chopped
- 1 carrot, chopped
- 4 tablespoons green olives, pitted
- 2 tablespoons pine nuts
- 14 ounces tomatoes, chopped
- 4 tablespoons chicken stock
- 4 Medjool dates, chopped
- 1/2 lemon, cut into wedges

Directions:

1. In a bowl, mix the chicken, salt, pepper, oil, cumin, paprika and coriander and toss.
2. Take your 3-Quart Instant Pot; open the top lid. Plug it and turn it on.
3. Press "SAUTÉ" setting and the pot will start heating up.
4. In the cooking pot area, add the meat. Stir and cook until evenly brown from all sides for 4-5 minutes.
5. Add the garlic, onion, carrot, tomatoes, stock, dates and olives; stir gently.
6. Close the top lid and seal its valve.
7. Press "MANUAL" setting. Adjust cooking time to 20 minutes.
8. Allow the recipe to cook for the set cooking time.

9. After the set cooking time ends, press "CANCEL" and then press "QPR (Quick Pressure Release)".
10. Instant Pot will quickly release the pressure.
11. Open the top lid, add the cooked recipe mix in serving plates.
12. Serve with mint and pine nuts on top and enjoy!

Nutritional Values (Per Serving):

Calories - 454

Fat – 27.5g

Carbohydrates – 16g

Fiber – 4g

Protein – 31.5g

Maple Tomato Chicken

Prep Time: 5-8 min.

Cooking Time: 10 min.

Number of Servings: 2

Ingredients:

- 2 red onions, chopped
- 2 garlic cloves, minced
- 2 chicken breasts, boneless and skinless
- 2 tomatoes, chopped
- 1 tablespoon maple syrup
- 1 teaspoon chili powder
- 1 cup water
- 1 teaspoon cloves
- 1 teaspoon basil, dried

Directions:

1. Take your 3-Quart Instant Pot; open the top lid. Plug it and turn it on.
2. In the cooking pot area, add the tomatoes, onions, chicken, garlic, maple syrup, chili powder, basil, water, and cloves. Using a spatula, stir the ingredients.
3. Close the top lid and seal its valve.
4. Press "MANUAL" setting. Adjust cooking time to 10 minutes.
5. Allow the recipe to cook for the set cooking time.
6. After the set cooking time ends, press "CANCEL" and then press "QPR (Quick Pressure Release)".
7. Instant Pot will quickly release the pressure.
8. Open the top lid, take out the meat and shred it.
9. Add back to the mix and combine; add the cooked recipe mix in serving plates.
10. Serve and enjoy!

Nutritional Values (Per Serving):

Calories – 269

Fat – 5.5g

Carbohydrates – 17g

Fiber – 2.5g

Protein – 26.5g

Couple's BBQ Chicken

Prep Time: 8-10 min.

Cooking Time: 10 min.

Number of Servings: 2

Ingredients:

- 1 cup water
- ½ cup chopped onion
- 2-½ tablespoons raw honey
- ½ cup barbecue sauce
- ¼ teaspoon salt
- ½ teaspoon pepper
- 2 pounds chicken wings

Directions:

1. Take your 3-Quart Instant Pot; open the top lid. Plug it and turn it on.
2. In the cooking pot area, add the ingredients. Using a spatula, stir the ingredients.
3. Close the top lid and seal its valve.
4. Press "MANUAL" setting. Adjust cooking time to 10 minutes.
5. Allow the recipe to cook for the set cooking time.
6. After the set cooking time ends, press "CANCEL" and then press "QPR (Quick Pressure Release)".
7. Instant Pot will quickly release the pressure.
8. Open the pot and add the mixture in a saucepan.
9. Cook for a few minutes to thicken the sauce.
10. Serve and enjoy!

Nutritional Values (Per Serving):

Calories – 309

Fat – 9g

Carbohydrates – 47g

Fiber – 2g

Protein – 11g

Mexican Style Pepper Turkey

Prep Time: 5-8 min.

Cooking Time: 20 min.

Number of Servings: 3

Ingredients:

- 1/2 cup chicken stock
- 1 clove garlic, chopped
- 1 pound turkey breast, ground
- ½ tablespoon butter
- 1/2 red onion, sliced
- 1 cup canned diced tomatoes
- 1/2 red bell pepper, chopped
- 1/2 green bell pepper, chopped

Directions:

1. Take your 3-Quart Instant Pot; open the top lid. Plug it and turn it on.
2. Press "SAUTÉ" setting and the pot will start heating up.
3. In the cooking pot area, add the butter and meat. Stir and cook for 5 minutes to soften.
4. Mix in the tomatoes with their juices, garlic, onion, peppers, and stock.
5. Close the top lid and seal its valve.
6. Press "MANUAL" setting. Adjust cooking time to 8 minutes.
7. Allow the recipe to cook for the set cooking time.
8. After the set cooking time ends, press "CANCEL" and then press "QPR (Quick Pressure Release)".
9. Instant Pot will quickly release the pressure.
10. Open the top lid, add the cooked recipe mix in serving plates.
11. Serve and enjoy!

Nutritional Values (Per Serving):

Calories – 342

Fat – 11.5g

Carbohydrates – 14g

Fiber – 3g

Protein – 44.5g

Tangy Olive Chicken

Prep Time: 8-10 min.

Cooking Time: 13 min.

Number of Servings: 2

Ingredients:

- 3 tablespoons butter
- Juice from 1/2 lemon
- A pinch of cumin, ground
- 2 chicken breasts, skinless and boneless
- 1/2 cup green olives, pitted
- 3 tablespoons red onion, chopped
- A pinch of pepper and salt
- 2 lemon slices
- 1/2 cup chicken stock

Directions:

1. Take your 3-Quart Instant Pot; open the top lid. Plug it and turn it on.
2. Press "SAUTÉ" setting and the pot will start heating up.
3. In the cooking pot area, add the chicken breasts, season with salt, pepper, and cumin.
4. Cook and brown for 3 minutes on each side.
5. Add the butter, lemon juice, lemon slices, stock, olives, and onion; gently stir.
6. Close the top lid and seal its valve.
7. Press "MANUAL" setting. Adjust cooking time to 10 minutes.
8. Allow the recipe to cook for the set cooking time.
9. After the set cooking time ends, press "CANCEL" and then press "QPR (Quick Pressure Release)".
10. Instant Pot will quickly release the pressure.
11. Open the top lid, add the cooked recipe mix in serving plates.
12. Serve and enjoy!

Nutritional Values (Per Serving):

Calories – 423

Fat – 27.5g

Carbohydrates – 15g

Fiber – 2g

Protein – 27.5g

Chapter 5: Beef, Lamb & Pork

Green Chili Beef

Prep Time: 8-10 min.

Cooking Time: 60 min.

Number of Servings: 2

Ingredients:

- 1 pound beef roast, make medium size cubes
- 2 garlic cloves, minced
- 1 tablespoon coconut vinegar
- 2 ounces green chilies, chopped
- 1 teaspoon oregano, dried
- A pinch of pepper and salt
- 2 teaspoons cumin, ground
- 1/2 cup water
- 1 small yellow onion, chopped
- 1 chipotle pepper, chopped
- Juice from 1 lime

Directions:

1. Take your 3-Quart Instant Pot; open the top lid. Plug it and turn it on.
2. In the cooking pot area, add the garlic, onion, green chilies, beef, oregano, salt, pepper, chipotle pepper, lime juice, vinegar, cumin and water. Using a spatula, stir the ingredients.
3. Close the top lid and seal its valve.
4. Press "MANUAL" setting. Adjust cooking time to 60 minutes.
5. Allow the recipe to cook for the set cooking time.
6. After the set cooking time ends, press "CANCEL" and then press "QPR (Quick Pressure Release)".
7. Instant Pot will quickly release the pressure.
8. Open the top lid, add the cooked recipe mix in serving plates.
9. Serve and enjoy!

Nutritional Values (Per Serving):

Calories – 456

Fat – 22g

Carbohydrates – 32.5g

Fiber – 2g

Protein – 46.5g

Beef Red Potato Stew

Prep Time: 8-10 min.

Cooking Time: 25 min.

Number of Servings: 2

Ingredients:

- 1 pound beef meat, make medium size cubes
- 1 tablespoon olive oil
- 2 tablespoons parsley, chopped
- 3 tablespoons beef broth
- 1 tablespoon flour
- 1/2 tablespoon tomato paste
- A pinch of pepper and salt
- 1 small yellow onion, chopped
- 1 garlic clove, crushed or minced
- 1 cup beef stock
- 1 celery stalk, chopped
- 2 small carrots, chopped
- 1/2 pound red potatoes, chopped

Directions:

1. In a bowl, mix the beef meat, salt, pepper and flour and toss.
2. Take your 3-Quart Instant Pot; open the top lid. Plug it and turn it on.
3. Press "SAUTÉ" setting and the pot will start heating up.
4. In the cooking pot area, add the oil and meat. Stir and cook until evenly brown from all sides.
5. Add the beef broth and cook for 2 minutes.
6. Add the carrots, garlic, onions, potatoes, celery, stock and tomato paste, stir gently.
7. Close the top lid and seal its valve.
8. Press "MANUAL" setting. Adjust cooking time to 20 minutes.
9. Allow the recipe to cook for the set cooking time.
10. After the set cooking time ends, press "CANCEL" and then press "QPR (Quick Pressure Release)".
11. Instant Pot will quickly release the pressure.

12. Open the top lid, add the cooked recipe mix in serving plates.
13. Serve top with some parsley and enjoy!

Nutritional Values (Per Serving):

Calories - 515

Fat – 18.5g

Carbohydrates – 29g

Fiber – 4g

Protein – 52.5g

Spiced Potato Lamb Dinner

Prep Time: 10 min.

Cooking Time: 35 min.

Number of Servings: 2-3

Ingredients:

- 1 tomato, chopped
- 1/2 pound rack of lamb
- 1/2 pound baby potatoes
- 1 carrot, chopped
- 1 cup chicken stock
- 1/2 onion, chopped
- 1 celery stalk, chopped
- A pinch of rosemary, dried
- 1 tablespoon ketchup
- 1 tablespoon beef broth
- 2 garlic cloves, minced
- A pinch of pepper and salt
- 1 teaspoon sweet paprika
- 1 teaspoon cumin, ground
- A pinch of oregano, dried

Directions:

1. Take your 3-Quart Instant Pot; open the top lid. Plug it and turn it on.
2. In the cooking pot area, add the baby potatoes, carrot, onion, celery, tomato, stock, garlic, salt, pepper, paprika, cumin, oregano, rosemary, ketchup, lamb, and beef broth. Using a spatula, stir the ingredients.
3. Close the top lid and seal its valve.
4. Press "MANUAL" setting. Adjust cooking time to 35 minutes.
5. Allow the recipe to cook for the set cooking time.
6. After the set cooking time ends, press "CANCEL" and then press "QPR (Quick Pressure Release)".
7. Instant Pot will quickly release the pressure.
8. Open the top lid, add the cooked recipe mix in serving plates.
9. Serve and enjoy!

Nutritional Values (Per Serving):

Calories – 371

Fat – 13.5g

Carbohydrates – 32g

Fiber – 3g

Protein – 33.5g

Pork Meatball Curry

Prep Time: 10-15 min.

Cooking Time: 25 min.

Number of Servings: 2-3

Ingredients:

- ¼ cup coconut milk
- ¾ teaspoon brown sugar
- 1 tablespoon breadcrumb
- ¾ pounds pork, ground
- ¼ cup chopped onion
- 1 egg, medium size

Directions:

1. Mix the pork with egg and breadcrumbs. Shape the mixture into balls.
2. Take your 3-Quart Instant Pot; open the top lid. Plug it and turn it on.
3. Press "SAUTÉ" setting and the pot will start heating up.
4. In the cooking pot area, add the milk, meatballs, onions and sugar; stir gently.
5. Close the top lid and seal its valve.
6. Press "MANUAL" setting. Adjust cooking time to 25 minutes.
7. Allow the recipe to cook for the set cooking time.
8. After the set cooking time ends, press "CANCEL" and then press "NPR (Natural Pressure Release)".
9. Instant Pot will slowly and naturally release the pressure.
10. Open the top lid, add the cooked recipe mix in serving plates.
11. Serve and enjoy!

Nutritional Values (Per Serving):

Calories – 247

Fat – 19.5g

Carbohydrates – 8g

Fiber – 2g

Protein – 14.5g

Squash Wine Lamb Meal

Prep Time: 10 min.

Cooking Time: 50 min.

Number of Servings: 2-3

Ingredients:

- ½ butternut squash, make medium size cubes
- 1 small onion, chopped
- 2 parsnips, make medium size cubes
- 2 cloves garlic crushed
- ¼ cup white wine
- ¼ cup stock
- Olive oil as needed
- Pepper and salt as needed
- ¾ pound lamb
- 2 carrots, make medium size cubes

Directions:

1. Take your 3-Quart Instant Pot; open the top lid. Plug it and turn it on.
2. Press "SAUTÉ" setting and the pot will start heating up.
3. In the cooking pot area, add the meat. Stir and cook until evenly brown from all sides.
4. Add rest the ingredients and stir gently.
5. Close the top lid and seal its valve.
6. Press "MEAT/STEW" setting. Adjust cooking time to 45 minutes.
7. Allow the recipe to cook for the set cooking time.
8. After the set cooking time ends, press "CANCEL" and then press "QPR (Quick Pressure Release)".
9. Instant Pot will quickly release the pressure.
10. Open the top lid, take out the meat and shred it.
11. Add back to the mix and combine; add the cooked recipe mix in serving plates.
12. Serve and enjoy!

Nutritional Values (Per Serving):

Calories - 486

Fat – 29.5g

Carbohydrates – 43.5g

Fiber – 13.5g

Protein – 39g

Artichoke Mayo Beef

Prep Time: 10 min.

Cooking Time: 15 min.

Number of Servings: 2

Ingredients:

- 1 pound beef, ground
- 1 small yellow onion, chopped
- 1/2 teaspoon dill, dried
- 1/2 teaspoon apple cider vinegar
- 3 tablespoons mayonnaise
- 1/2 teaspoon garlic powder
- 1/2 teaspoon oregano, dried
- 1/2 tablespoon olive oil
- 1/3 cup water
- 1/2 teaspoon onion powder
- A pinch of pepper and salt
- 1 ¼ cup artichoke hearts

Directions:

1. Take your 3-Quart Instant Pot; open the top lid. Plug it and turn it on.
2. Press "SAUTÉ" setting and the pot will start heating up.
3. In the cooking pot area, add the oil and onions. Cook until starts becoming translucent and softened for 3 minutes. Stir in between.
4. Add the beef, salt, pepper, oregano, dill, garlic and onion powder, stir and cook for 3 minutes.
5. Add water and artichokes; stir gently.
6. Close the top lid and seal its valve.
7. Press "MANUAL" setting. Adjust cooking time to 7 minutes.
8. Allow the recipe to cook for the set cooking time.
9. After the set cooking time ends, press "CANCEL" and then press "QPR (Quick Pressure Release)".
10. Instant Pot will quickly release the pressure.
11. Open the top lid, add the cooked recipe mix in serving plates.
12. Drain excess water, mix the vinegar and mayo.

13. Serve and enjoy!

Nutritional Values (Per Serving):

Calories - 544

Fat – 19g

Carbohydrates – 48.5g

Fiber – 7g

Protein – 41g

Apple Pork Roast

Prep Time: 5-8 min.

Cooking Time: 30 min.

Number of Servings: 2

Ingredients:

- 1/2 tablespoon olive oil
- A pinch of onion powder
- 1-pound pork roast
- A pinch of pepper and salt
- 1 cup water
- A pinch of chili powder
- A pinch of garlic powder
- 3 tablespoons apple juice

Directions:

1. In a bowl, mix the chili powder, onion powder, roast, garlic powder, salt, and pepper.
2. Take your 3-Quart Instant Pot; open the top lid. Plug it and turn it on.
3. Press "SAUTÉ" setting and the pot will start heating up.
4. In the cooking pot area, add the oil and meat mix. Stir and cook until evenly brown from all sides for 4-5 minutes.
5. Add the apple juice and water.
6. Close the top lid and seal its valve.
7. Press "MANUAL" setting. Adjust cooking time to 25 minutes.
8. Allow the recipe to cook for the set cooking time.
9. After the set cooking time ends, press "CANCEL" and then press "QPR (Quick Pressure Release)".
10. Instant Pot will quickly release the pressure.
11. Open the top lid, take out the meat and slice it.
12. Add back to the mix and combine; add the cooked recipe mix in serving plates.
13. Serve and enjoy!

Nutritional Values (Per Serving):

Calories - 133

Fat – 12.5g

Carbohydrates – 4g

Fiber – 0g

Protein – 3g

Sweet Soy Salmon

Prep Time: 8-10 min.

Cooking Time: 7 min.

Number of Servings: 2

Ingredients:

- 2 tablespoons soy sauce
- ¾ pound salmon fillets
- 1 teaspoon vegetable oil
- 1 tablespoon lemon juice
- ¼ teaspoon pepper
- 2 tablespoons brown sugar
- 1 tablespoon fish sauce
- ¼ teaspoon lemon zest
- ½ teaspoon ginger

Directions:

1. Season the salmon with pepper and salt. Set aside.
2. In a bowl, mix the oil, sugar, fish sauce, soy sauce, ginger, lemon zest, and lemon juice.
3. Take your 3-Quart Instant Pot; open the top lid. Plug it and turn it on.
4. Press "SAUTÉ" setting and the pot will start heating up.
5. In the cooking pot area, add the bowl mix and cook for 2 minutes to caramelize. Add the salmon.
6. Close the top lid and seal its valve.
7. Press "MANUAL" setting. Adjust cooking time to 5 minutes.
8. Allow the recipe to cook for the set cooking time.
9. After the set cooking time ends, press "CANCEL" and then press "NPR (Natural Pressure Release)".
10. Instant Pot will slowly and naturally release the pressure.
11. Open the top lid, add the cooked recipe mix in serving plates.
12. Serve with some green vegetables of your choice and enjoy!

Nutritional Values (Per Serving):

Calories - 257

Fat – 13.5g

Carbohydrates – 21g

Fiber – 3g

Protein – 14.5g

Orangy Cod Dinner

Prep Time: 5-8 min.

Cooking Time: 7 min.

Number of Servings: 2

Ingredients:

- 1/2 cup fish stock
- A pinch of pepper and salt
- 2 cod fillets, boneless
- A drizzle of olive oil
- 1-inch ginger, grated
- Zest and juice from 1/2 orange
- 2 sprigs onions, chopped
- More orange juice to drizzle

Directions:

1. Season the cod with salt and pepper, drizzle oil and rub well.
2. Take your 3-Quart Instant Pot; open the top lid. Plug it and turn it on.
3. Add the stock with orange zest, juice, ginger and sprigs onions and place steamer basket/trivet inside the pot; arrange the seasoned cod over the basket/trivet.
4. Close the top lid and seal its valve.
5. Press "MANUAL" setting. Adjust cooking time to 7 minutes.
6. Allow the recipe to cook for the set cooking time.
7. After the set cooking time ends, press "CANCEL" and then press "QPR (Quick Pressure Release)".
8. Instant Pot will quickly release the pressure.
9. Open the top lid, add the cooked recipe mix in serving plates.
10. Serve with some more orange juice on top and enjoy!

Nutritional Values (Per Serving):

Calories - 186

Fat – 4.5g

Carbohydrates – 16g

Fiber – 4g

Protein – 3g

Broccoli Salmon Meal

Prep Time: 8-10 min.

Cooking Time: 6 min.

Number of Servings: 2

Ingredients:

- 1 cinnamon stick
- 2 salmon fillets, boneless and skin on
- 2 cups broccoli florets
- 1 bay leaf
- 1 tablespoon olive oil
- 1 cup water
- 3 cloves
- Some lime wedges for serving
- 1 cup baby carrots
- 1 pinch of pepper and salt

Directions:

1. In a bowl, season the salmon with salt and pepper, brush it with the oil and mix with carrots and broccoli.
2. Take your 3-Quart Instant Pot; open the top lid. Plug it and turn it on.
3. Pour the cinnamon, cloves, bay leaf and water and place steamer basket/trivet inside the pot; arrange the salmon mix over the basket/trivet.
4. Close the top lid and seal its valve.
5. Press "MANUAL" setting. Adjust cooking time to 6 minutes.
6. Allow the recipe to cook for the set cooking time.
7. After the set cooking time ends, press "CANCEL" and then press "QPR (Quick Pressure Release)".
8. Instant Pot will quickly release the pressure.
9. Open the top lid, add the cooked recipe mix in serving plates.
10. Discard bay leaf, cloves and cinnamon.
11. Serve with some lime wedges and enjoy!

Nutritional Values (Per Serving):

Calories – 363

Fat – 22.5g

Carbohydrates – 15g

Fiber – 5g

Protein – 29g

Shrimp Pasta Meal

Prep Time: 8-10 min.

Cooking Time: 3 min.

Number of Servings: 2-3

Ingredients:

- 1 pound shrimp
- 1 tablespoon olive oil
- 1 tablespoon butter
- 1/2 tablespoon garlic, minced
- 1/4 cup chicken broth
- A pinch of pepper and salt
- Your favorite pasta, cooked
- 1/4 cup chicken stock
- 1/2 tablespoon lemon juice
- 1 tablespoon parsley, chopped

Directions:

1. Take your 3-Quart Instant Pot; open the top lid. Plug it and turn it on.
2. Press "SAUTÉ" setting and the pot will start heating up.
3. In the cooking pot area, add the oil and butter; heat it.
4. Add the garlic; cook until starts becoming translucent and softened for 1 minutes. Stir in between.
5. Add the stock and chicken broth; add the shrimp and parsley.
6. Close the top lid and seal its valve.
7. Press "MANUAL" setting. Adjust cooking time to 2 minutes.
8. Allow the recipe to cook for the set cooking time.
9. After the set cooking time ends, press "CANCEL" and then press "QPR (Quick Pressure Release)".
10. Instant Pot will quickly release the pressure.
11. Open the top lid, add the cooked recipe mix in serving plates.
12. Serve with cooked pasta and enjoy!

Nutritional Values (Per Serving):

Calories – 468

Fat – 17.5g

Carbohydrates – 36g

Fiber – 7g

Protein – 41g

Fish Coconut Curry

Prep Time: 5-8 min.

Cooking Time: 7-8 min.

Number of Servings: 2

Ingredients:

- 1 pound fish fillets, make small chunks
- 1 tablespoon oil
- ¼ teaspoon turmeric powder
- ¼ teaspoon ground fenugreek
- 1 tomato, chopped
- 1 bell pepper, thinly sliced
- 2 cloves garlic, crushed
- ¼ teaspoon chili powder
- 1 teaspoon ground cumin
- 1 teaspoon ginger, grated
- 1 teaspoon ground coriander
- 1 cup coconut milk
- 1 tablespoon lemon juice
- A handful curry leaves
- Salt as needed

Directions:

1. Take your 3-Quart Instant Pot; open the top lid. Plug it and turn it on.
2. Press "SAUTÉ" setting and the pot will start heating up.
3. In the cooking pot area, add the oil and curry leaves.
4. Mix in the onion, ginger, and garlic, cook to soften and translucent.
5. Add all the spices and sauté for a few seconds until the mixture becomes fragrant.
6. Add remaining ingredients except for lemon juice; gently stir the mix.
7. Close the top lid and seal its valve.
8. Press "MANUAL" setting. Adjust cooking time to 5 minutes.
9. Allow the recipe to cook for the set cooking time.

10. After the set cooking time ends, press "CANCEL" and then press "QPR (Quick Pressure Release)".
11. Instant Pot will quickly release the pressure.
12. Open the top lid, add the cooked recipe mix in serving plates.
13. Mix in the lemon juice and enjoy!

Nutritional Values (Per Serving):

Calories – 423

Fat – 23.5g

Carbohydrates – 29.5g

Fiber – 8g

Protein – 14g

Garlic Chili Salmon

Prep Time: 5-8 min.

Cooking Time: 5 min.

Number of Servings: 2

Ingredients:

- 2 salmon fillets
- 1 cup water
- Juice from 1 lime
- 1/2 teaspoon cumin, ground
- A pinch of pepper and salt
- 1 jalapeno, chopped
- 2 garlic cloves, minced
- 1 tablespoon honey
- 1 tablespoon hot water
- 1/2 teaspoon sweet paprika
- 1 tablespoon olive oil
- 1 tablespoon parsley, chopped
- Chili sauce as needed

Directions:

1. In a bowl, mix the jalapeno with lime juice, garlic, honey, oil, 1 tablespoon water, parsley, paprika and cumin. Whisk the mix.
2. Take your 3-Quart Instant Pot; open the top lid. Plug it and turn it on.
3. Pour 1 cup water and place steamer basket/trivet inside the pot; arrange the salmon over the basket/trivet. Season the salmon with pepper and salt.
4. Close the top lid and seal its valve.
5. Press "STEAM" setting. Adjust cooking time to 5 minutes.
6. Allow the recipe to cook for the set cooking time.
7. After the set cooking time ends, press "CANCEL" and then press "QPR (Quick Pressure Release)".
8. Instant Pot will quickly release the pressure.
9. Open the top lid, add the cooked recipe mix in serving plates.
10. Add the sauce on top. Serve and enjoy!

Nutritional Values (Per Serving):

Calories - 347

Fat – 21g

Carbohydrates – 18.5g

Fiber – 3g

Protein – 28g

Kidney Bean Sausage Risotto

Prep Time: 10-15 min.

Cooking Time: 44 min.

Number of Servings: 2

Ingredients:

- 1/3 pound red kidney beans
- 1/2 yellow onion, chopped
- 1 small red bell pepper, chopped
- A pinch of pepper and salt
- A pinch of white pepper
- 1 celery stalk, chopped
- 3 cup water
- 1 garlic clove, crushed or minced
- 1/2 teaspoon thyme, chopped
- 1/2 pound chicken sausage, sliced
- 3 cup rice, cooked
- 1/3 teaspoon hot sauce
- 1 bay leaf

Directions:

1. Take your 3-Quart Instant Pot; open the top lid. Plug it and turn it on.
2. In the cooking pot area, add the bell pepper, celery, onion, garlic, beans, salt, black pepper, white pepper, thyme, hot sauce, bay leaf, and water. Using a spatula, stir the ingredients.
3. Close the top lid and seal its valve.
4. Press "MANUAL" setting. Adjust cooking time to 28 minutes.
5. Allow the recipe to cook for the set cooking time.
6. After the set cooking time ends, press "CANCEL" and then press "QPR (Quick Pressure Release)".
7. Instant Pot will quickly release the pressure.
8. Add the sausage, stir gently.

9. Close the top lid and seal its valve.
10. Press "MANUAL" setting. Adjust cooking time to 15 minutes.
11. Allow the recipe to cook for the set cooking time.
12. After the set cooking time ends, press "CANCEL" and then press "QPR (Quick Pressure Release)".
13. Instant Pot will quickly release the pressure.
14. Divide rice on 2 plates, add the beans mix on top and serve.

Nutritional Values (Per Serving):

Calories – 403

Fat – 11g

Carbohydrates – 49g

Fiber – 8g

Protein – 18.5g

Tangy Asparagus Risotto

Prep Time: 5 min.

Cooking Time: 10 min.

Number of Servings: 2-3

Ingredients:

- ¼ cup parmesan, grated
- 2 tablespoons orange juice
- ½ cup risotto rice
- 2 garlic cloves, chopped
- 1 small onion, chopped
- ½ pound diced asparagus
- 1 1/3 cup vegetable stock
- 1 tablespoon olive oil
- 1 tablespoon thyme

Directions:

1. Take your 3-Quart Instant Pot; open the top lid. Plug it and turn it on.
2. Press "SAUTÉ" setting and the pot will start heating up.
3. In the cooking pot area, add the oil and onions. Cook until starts becoming translucent and softened. Stir in between.
4. Mix the rice and the garlic, cook until the garlic becomes fragrant. Mix in the stock and the orange juice.
5. Close the top lid and seal its valve.
6. Press "MANUAL" setting. Adjust cooking time to 7 minutes.
7. Allow the recipe to cook for the set cooking time.
8. After the set cooking time ends, press "CANCEL" and then press "QPR (Quick Pressure Release)".
9. Instant Pot will quickly release the pressure.
10. Add the thyme and asparagus; combine gently. Do not cover, let it sit for 8 minutes for asparagus to soften.
11. Open the top lid, add the cooked recipe mix in serving plates.
12. Serve with the cheese on top and enjoy!

Nutritional Values (Per Serving):

Calories - 421

Fat – 14.5g

Carbohydrates – 42g

Fiber – 4.5g

Protein – 22g

Spiced Chickpea Curry

Prep Time: 8-10 min.

Cooking Time: 18 min.

Number of Servings: 2

Ingredients:

- 1 cup chickpeas, soaked overnight or 7-8 hours and drained
- ½ cup spinach, chopped
- 1 cup water
- 1/2 cup tomatoes, chopped
- 1 tablespoon olive oil
- 4 tablespoons red onion, chopped
- 1 garlic clove, crushed or minced
- A pinch of turmeric powder
- 1 bay leaf
- 1/2 tablespoon curry powder
- A pinch of chili powder
- A pinch of garam masala
- 1/2 tablespoon lemon juice
- A pinch of pepper and salt
- 1 tablespoon cilantro, chopped

Directions:

1. Take your 3-Quart Instant Pot; open the top lid. Plug it and turn it on.
2. Press "SAUTÉ" setting and the pot will start heating up.
3. In the cooking pot area, add the oil, garlic, and onions. Cook until starts becoming translucent and softened for 2-3 minutes. Stir in between.
4. Add the tomatoes, stir and cook for 4 minutes more.
5. Add the chili powder, garam masala, turmeric, bay leaf and curry powder, stir and cook for 1 minute more.
6. Add chickpeas, spinach and water, stir gently.
7. Close the top lid and seal its valve.
8. Press "MANUAL" setting. Adjust cooking time to 10 minutes.
9. Allow the recipe to cook for the set cooking time.

10. After the set cooking time ends, press "CANCEL" and then press "QPR (Quick Pressure Release)".
11. Instant Pot will quickly release the pressure.
12. Open the top lid, add the cooked recipe mix in serving plates.
13. Discard the bay leaf, mix the lemon juice and cilantro, some salt and pepper.
14. Serve and enjoy!

Nutritional Values (Per Serving):

Calories - 452

Fat – 13.5g

Carbohydrates – 52.5g

Fiber – 17g

Protein – 21g

Brown Rice Ham Treat

Prep Time: 5 min.

Cooking Time: 6 min.

Number of Servings: 2-3

Ingredients:

- ½ cup ham, diced
- 2 tablespoons scallions, sliced
- ½ cup carrots, make matchsticks
- 1 ½ cup brown rice
- 1 tablespoon butter
- 1 ½ cup water
- 1 tablespoon soy sauce

Directions:

1. Take your 3-Quart Instant Pot; open the top lid. Plug it and turn it on.
2. In the cooking pot area, add the ingredients. Using a spatula, stir the ingredients.
3. Close the top lid and seal its valve.
4. Press "MANUAL" setting. Adjust cooking time to 6 minutes.
5. Allow the recipe to cook for the set cooking time.
6. After the set cooking time ends, press "CANCEL" and then press "QPR (Quick Pressure Release)".
7. Instant Pot will quickly release the pressure.
8. Open the top lid, fluff the rice and add the cooked recipe mix in serving plates.
9. Serve and enjoy!
10. Ensure that the rice is tender and has there is no liquid left in the pot. If the rice is not tender, cook for a few more minutes.

Nutritional Values (Per Serving):

Calories - 128

Fat – 6.5g

Carbohydrates – 11g

Fiber – 2g

Protein – 4g

BBQ Lentil Meal

Prep Time: 8-10 min.

Cooking Time: 15 min.

Number of Servings: 2

Ingredients:

- 1 tomato, make rounds
- Toasted bread to serve
- ½ cucumber, make rounds
- ¼ cup BBQ sauce

For lentils:
- 1 cup water
- ½ cup green lentils, soaked overnight and drained

Directions:

1. Take your 3-Quart Instant Pot; open the top lid. Plug it and turn it on.
2. In the cooking pot area, add the lentils and water. Using a spatula, stir the ingredients.
3. Close the top lid and seal its valve.
4. Press "MANUAL" setting. Adjust cooking time to 15 minutes.
5. Allow the recipe to cook for the set cooking time.
6. After the set cooking time ends, press "CANCEL" and then press "NPR (Natural Pressure Release)".
7. Instant Pot will slowly and naturally release the pressure.
8. Open the top lid, add the BBQ sauce and mix well.
9. Arrange the mix over toasted bread. On top of the breads, add sliced tomatoes and cucumber.
10. Serve and enjoy!

Nutritional Values (Per Serving):

Calories - 136

Fat – 1g

Carbohydrates – 22g

Fiber – 3g

Protein – 5.5g

Mexican Bean Avocado Rice

Prep Time: 10-15 min.

Cooking Time: 28 min.

Number of Servings: 2-3

Ingredients:

- 2 garlic cloves, minced
- 1 lime, make wedges
- 1 avocado, pitted, peeled and sliced
- 1 cup black beans, washed
- 1/2 cup onion, chopped
- 1 cup brown rice
- 4 1/2 cup water
- A pinch of salt

Directions:

1. Take your 3-Quart Instant Pot; open the top lid. Plug it and turn it on.
2. In the cooking pot area, add the beans, water, rice, salt, garlic and onion. Using a spatula, stir the ingredients.
3. Close the top lid and seal its valve.
4. Press "MANUAL" setting. Adjust cooking time to 28 minutes.
5. Allow the recipe to cook for the set cooking time.
6. After the set cooking time ends, press "CANCEL" and then press "QPR (Quick Pressure Release)".
7. Instant Pot will quickly release the pressure.
8. Open the top lid, add the cooked recipe mix in serving plates.
9. Serve with lime wedges and avocado slices.

Nutritional Values (Per Serving):

Calories – 336

Fat – 13.5g

Carbohydrates – 36g

Fiber – 12g

Protein – 13.5g

Spinach Lentil Soup

Prep Time: 10 min.

Cooking Time: 18 min.

Number of Servings: 2

Ingredients:

- 1/2 teaspoon turmeric, ground
- 1 teaspoon olive oil
- 1/2 cup yellow onion, chopped
- 1/3 cup celery, chopped
- 1 tablespoon garlic, minced
- 3 cup baby spinach
- 1/2 cup carrot, chopped
- 1 teaspoon cumin, ground
- 2 cup veggie stock
- 1/2 cup lentils
- 1/2 teaspoon thyme, dried
- A pinch of pepper and salt

Directions:

1. Take your 3-Quart Instant Pot; open the top lid. Plug it and turn it on.
2. Press "SAUTÉ" setting and the pot will start heating up.
3. In the cooking pot area, add the oil, carrot, celery, and onions.
4. Stir and cook for 5 minutes.
5. Mix the turmeric, garlic, cumin, thyme, salt, and pepper, and cook for 1 minute more.
6. Mix the lentils and stock.
7. Close the top lid and seal its valve.
8. Press "MANUAL" setting. Adjust cooking time to 12 minutes.
9. Allow the recipe to cook for the set cooking time.
10. After the set cooking time ends, press "CANCEL" and then press "QPR (Quick Pressure Release)".

11. Instant Pot will quickly release the pressure.
12. Open the top lid, add the cooked recipe mix in serving bowls.
13. Mix the spinach. Serve and enjoy!

Nutritional Values (Per Serving):

Calories – 121

Fat – 3g

Carbohydrates – 17.5g

Fiber – 7g

Protein – 7.5g

Cheesy Tomato Soup

Prep Time: 10-15 min.

Cooking Time: 28 min.

Number of Servings: 2-3

Ingredients:

- 2 cups of chopped ripe tomatoes
- 2 tablespoons tomato paste
- 3 tablespoons olive oil, extra virgin
- 2 medium onions, chopped
- 2 medium carrots, peeled and chopped
- 3 large garlic cloves, finely chopped
- 1 tablespoon sugar
- 1 cup vegetable broth
- Pepper and salt as needed
- 1/2 cup Parmesan cheese, grated
- 1/2 cup heavy cream
- 4 basil leaves, as a garnish

Directions:

1. Take your 3-Quart Instant Pot; open the top lid. Plug it and turn it on.
2. Press "SAUTÉ" setting and the pot will start heating up.
3. In the cooking pot area, add the oil, carrot, and onions. Cook until starts becoming translucent and softened for 6-7 minutes. Stir in between.
4. Toss in the garlic and stir until fragrant.
5. Add in the tomato paste, tomatoes, broth, sugar, pepper and salt; stir gently.
6. Close the top lid and seal its valve.
7. Press "MANUAL" setting. Adjust cooking time to 20 minutes.
8. Allow the recipe to cook for the set cooking time.
9. After the set cooking time ends, press "CANCEL" and then press "NPR (Natural Pressure Release)".
10. Instant Pot will slowly and naturally release the pressure.
11. Open the top lid, add the cooked recipe mix in serving plates.
12. Pour in the cream, and puree the mix in a blender.
13. Garnish with torn basil leaves and cheese. Serve warm.

Nutritional Values (Per Serving):

Calories – 323

Fat – 27.5g

Carbohydrates – 12g

Fiber – 2g

Protein – 14g

Italian Sausage Cream Soup

Prep Time: 5-8 min.

Cooking Time: 12 min.

Number of Servings: 2-3

Ingredients:

- 1 small yellow onion, finely chopped
- ½ pound Italian sausages
- 1 large russet potato, washed and sliced
- 3 cups chicken broth
- ¼ cup heavy cream
- 1 tablespoon olive oil
- 2 cloves garlic, minced
- Pepper and salt as needed

Directions:

1. Take your 3-Quart Instant Pot; open the top lid. Plug it and turn it on.
2. Press "SAUTÉ" setting and the pot will start heating up.
3. In the cooking pot area, add the oil, garlic, and onions. Cook until starts becoming translucent and softened for 3 minutes. Stir in between.
4. Stir in the sausage and cook for an extra 3 minutes.
5. Mix the potato, broth, a pinch black pepper and salt.
6. Close the top lid and seal its valve.
7. Press "MANUAL" setting. Adjust cooking time to 6 minutes.
8. Allow the recipe to cook for the set cooking time.
9. After the set cooking time ends, press "CANCEL" and then press "QPR (Quick Pressure Release)".
10. Instant Pot will quickly release the pressure.
11. Open the top lid, add the cooked recipe mix in serving bowls.
12. Serve and enjoy!

Nutritional Values (Per Serving):

Calories - 623

Fat – 41g

Carbohydrates – 48.5g

Fiber – 14g

Protein – 42.5g

Marinara Turkey Soup

Prep Time: 8-10 min.

Cooking Time: 11 min.

Number of Servings: 2-3

Ingredients:

- 1/2 pound turkey, ground
- 1/2 tablespoon olive oil
- 1/2 cup cauliflower florets
- 1 garlic clove, crushed or minced
- 1/2 cup yellow onion, chopped
- 1/2 cabbage head, chopped
- 10 ounces marinara sauce
- 1 cup water
- 2 cups chicken stock

Directions:

1. Take your 3-Quart Instant Pot; open the top lid. Plug it and turn it on.
2. Press "SAUTÉ" setting and the pot will start heating up.
3. Add the oil, turkey, garlic, and onion, stir and sauté for 5 minutes.
4. Add the cauliflower, stock, water, marinara sauce and cabbage; stir gently.
5. Close the top lid and seal its valve.
6. Press "MANUAL" setting. Adjust cooking time to 6 minutes.
7. Allow the recipe to cook for the set cooking time.
8. After the set cooking time ends, press "CANCEL" and then press "QPR (Quick Pressure Release)".
9. Instant Pot will quickly release the pressure.
10. Open the top lid, add the cooked recipe mix in serving bowls.
11. Serve and enjoy!

Nutritional Values (Per Serving):

Calories – 309

Fat – 16.5g

Carbohydrates – 23g

Fiber – 4g

Protein – 16g

Chicken Spiced Tropical Soup

Prep Time: 8-10 min.

Cooking Time: 40 min.

Number of Servings: 2-3

Ingredients:

- 1 garlic clove, crushed or minced
- 1 small red onion, chopped
- 1 carrot, chopped
- Lime wedges for serving
- 1/2 small red cabbage, chopped
- A pinch of pepper and salt
- 1/2 pound chicken pieces
- 1/3 pineapple, peeled and make medium size cubes
- 1/2 teaspoon cinnamon powder
- 1/2 teaspoon turmeric powder
- 1 sprigs onion, chopped
- 1/2 teaspoon ginger powder
- 1/2 teaspoon white peppercorns
- 1/2 tablespoon tamarind paste
- Juice from 1/3 lime

Directions:

1. Take your 3-Quart Instant Pot; open the top lid. Plug it and turn it on.
2. In the cooking pot area, add the carrot, red onion, chicken, salt, pepper, cabbage, garlic, peppercorns. Using a spatula, stir the ingredients.
3. Close the top lid and seal its valve.
4. Press "SOUP" setting. Adjust cooking time to 30 minutes.
5. Allow the recipe to cook for the set cooking time.
6. After the set cooking time ends, press "CANCEL" and then press "QPR (Quick Pressure Release)".
7. Instant Pot will quickly release the pressure.
8. Open the top lid, take out the meat and shred it.
9. Add back to the mix and combine.

10. In a bowl, mix 1 tablespoon soup with tamarind paste, stir and pour into the pot mix.
11. Mix the cinnamon, ginger, turmeric, pineapple and lime juice; stir the mix.
12. Press "SAUTÉ" setting and cook for 10 minutes more.
13. Ladle into bowls, top with the sprigs onion on top and serve with lime wedges on the side.

Nutritional Values (Per Serving):

Calories – 427

Fat – 17g

Carbohydrates – 46.5g

Fiber – 18g

Protein – 11g

Wholesome Veggies Soup

Prep Time: 8-10 min.

Cooking Time: 8 min.

Number of Servings: 2-3

Ingredients:

- 2 tablespoons extra virgin olive oil
- 2 cloves garlic, crushed
- 2 large carrots, cut in 1/2 slices
- Pepper and salt, as needed
- 2 small potatoes, cut in ½-cubes
- 1 large onion, coarsely chopped
- 4 large zucchinis, cut in 1 slices
- 4 cups vegetable stock
- 1 tablespoon minced basil

Directions:

1. Take your 3-Quart Instant Pot; open the top lid. Plug it and turn it on.
2. Press "SAUTÉ" setting and the pot will start heating up.
3. In the cooking pot area, add the oil, garlic, and onions. Cook until starts becoming translucent and softened for 1 minutes. Stir in between.
4. Add the potatoes and sauté for another 1-2 minutes.
5. Add the remaining ingredients and stir to blend.
6. Close the top lid and seal its valve.
7. Press "MANUAL" setting. Adjust cooking time to 5 minutes.
8. Allow the recipe to cook for the set cooking time.
9. After the set cooking time ends, press "CANCEL" and then press "NPR (Natural Pressure Release)".
10. Instant Pot will slowly and naturally release the pressure.
11. Open the top lid, add the cooked recipe mix in serving plates.
12. Serve and enjoy!

Nutritional Values (Per Serving):

Calories - 358

Fat – 18.5g

Carbohydrates – 32g

Fiber – 9g

Protein – 6g

Super Garlic Potatoes

Prep Time: 8-10 min.

Cooking Time: 15 min.

Number of Servings: 2

Ingredients:

- 1/4 teaspoon onion powder
- A pinch of pepper and salt
- 2 tablespoons avocado oil
- 1/2 pound potatoes, cut into wedges
- 1/2 cup chicken stock
- 1/2 teaspoon garlic powder

Directions:

1. Take your 3-Quart Instant Pot; open the top lid. Plug it and turn it on.
2. Press "SAUTÉ" setting and the pot will start heating up.
3. In the cooking pot area, add the oil, potatoes, onion powder, garlic powder, salt and pepper, stir and cook for 8 minutes.
4. Add the stock, and stir.
5. Close the top lid and seal its valve.
6. Press "MANUAL" setting. Adjust cooking time to 7 minutes.
7. Allow the recipe to cook for the set cooking time.
8. After the set cooking time ends, press "CANCEL" and then press "QPR (Quick Pressure Release)".
9. Instant Pot will quickly release the pressure.
10. Open the top lid, add the cooked recipe mix in serving plates.
11. Serve and enjoy!

Nutritional Values (Per Serving):

Calories - 376

Fat – 8.5g

Carbohydrates – 47g

Fiber – 6g

Protein – 11g

Tomato Broccoli Treat

Prep Time: 8-10 min.

Cooking Time: 10 min.

Number of Servings: 2

Ingredients:

- ½ teaspoon nutmeg
- ¼ cup chopped onion
- ¼ teaspoon pepper
- 1 cup broccoli florets
- ¼ teaspoon salt
- 1 teaspoon olive oil
- 1 ½ cup tomato puree

Directions:

1. Take your 3-Quart Instant Pot; open the top lid. Plug it and turn it on.
2. Press "SAUTÉ" setting and the pot will start heating up.
3. In the cooking pot area, add the oil and onions. Cook until starts becoming translucent and softened. Stir in between.
4. Add the broccoli and tomato puree, mix in the nutmeg, pepper, and salt.
5. Close the top lid and seal its valve.
6. Press "MANUAL" setting. Adjust cooking time to 5 minutes.
7. Allow the recipe to cook for the set cooking time.
8. After the set cooking time ends, press "CANCEL" and then press "NPR (Natural Pressure Release)".
9. Instant Pot will slowly and naturally release the pressure.
10. Open the top lid, add the cooked recipe mix in serving plates.
11. Serve and enjoy!

Nutritional Values (Per Serving):

Calories - 126

Fat – 3.5g

Carbohydrates – 22g

Fiber – 5g

Protein – 5g

Vinegar-Braised Mushrooms

Prep Time: 5 min.

Cooking Time: 5 min.

Number of Servings: 2

Ingredients:

- 2 small garlic cloves, minced
- 1 1/2 tablespoon chicken broth
- 1/2 pound mushrooms, sliced
- 1 1/2 tablespoon olive oil
- A pinch of pepper and salt
- 1 1/2 tablespoon balsamic vinegar

Directions:

1. Take your 3-Quart Instant Pot; open the top lid. Plug it and turn it on.
2. Press "SAUTÉ" setting and the pot will start heating up.
3. In the cooking pot area, add the oil, garlic, and mushrooms. Cook until starts becoming translucent and softened for 3 minutes. Stir in between.
4. Add the chicken broth and vinegar, stir gently.
5. Close the top lid and seal its valve.
6. Press "MANUAL" setting. Adjust cooking time to 2 minutes.
7. Allow the recipe to cook for the set cooking time.
8. After the set cooking time ends, press "CANCEL" and then press "QPR (Quick Pressure Release)".
9. Instant Pot will quickly release the pressure.
10. Open the top lid, add the cooked recipe mix in serving plates.
11. Season as needed and enjoy!

Nutritional Values (Per Serving):

Calories - 153

Fat – 9g

Carbohydrates – 13.5g

Fiber – 1g

Protein – 3g

Kale Garlic Sides

Prep Time: 5 min.

Cooking Time: 5 min.

Number of Servings: 2-3

Ingredients:

- 1 cup water
- 1 teaspoon fish sauce
- ¼ teaspoon salt
- 2 cups chopped kale
- 1 teaspoon olive oil
- 3 teaspoon garlic
- 1 teaspoon oyster sauce (optional)

Directions:

1. Take your 3-Quart Instant Pot; open the top lid. Plug it and turn it on.
2. Press "SAUTÉ" setting and the pot will start heating up.
3. In the cooking pot area, add the oil and garlic. Cook until starts becoming translucent and softened for 2-3 minutes. Stir in between.
4. Add in the fish sauce, kale, water, oyster sauce, and salt.
5. Close the top lid and seal its valve.
6. Press "MANUAL" setting. Adjust cooking time to 3 minutes.
7. Allow the recipe to cook for the set cooking time.
8. After the set cooking time ends, press "CANCEL" and then press "NPR (Natural Pressure Release)".
9. Instant Pot will slowly and naturally release the pressure.
10. Open the top lid, add the cooked recipe mix in serving plates.
11. Serve and enjoy!

Nutritional Values (Per Serving):

Calories - 71

Fat – 3g

Carbohydrates – 7.5g

Fiber – 2g

Protein – 3g

Chapter 9: Mouthwatering Desserts

Tangy Blueberry Lemon Delight

Prep Time: 8-10 min.

Cooking Time: 8 min.

Number of Servings: 2

Ingredients:

- 1/4 cup lemon juice
- 3 egg yolks, whisked
- 2/3 cup sugar
- 2 cup blueberries
- 1 1/2 cup water
- 2 teaspoons lemon zest, grated
- 4 tablespoons butter

Directions:

1. Take your 3-Quart Instant Pot; open the top lid. Plug it and turn it on.
2. Press "SAUTÉ" setting and the pot will start heating up.
3. Add the lemon juice and blueberries, stir and simmer for 2 minutes.
4. Strain the mix into a bowl, mash the ingredients. Mix in the sugar, butter, lemon zest and egg yolks, whisk well and add the mix into two ramekins.
5. Pour the water and place steamer basket/trivet inside the pot; arrange the ramekins over the basket/trivet.
6. Close the top lid and seal its valve.
7. Press "MANUAL" setting. Adjust cooking time to 6 minutes.
8. Allow the recipe to cook for the set cooking time.
9. After the set cooking time ends, press "CANCEL" and then press "QPR (Quick Pressure Release)".
10. Instant Pot will quickly release the pressure.
11. Chill the ramekins in refrigerator and serve chilled.

Nutritional Values (Per Serving):

Calories - 413

Fat – 18.5g

Carbohydrates – 38g

Fiber – 6g

Protein – 4.5g

Cocoa Pudding Dessert

Prep Time: 8-10 min.

Cooking Time: 10-15 min.

Number of Servings: 2-3

Ingredients:

- 1 teaspoon vanilla extract
- 2 tablespoons cocoa powder
- 1 cup rice
- 5 cups coconut milk
- 1 cup sugar
- 1 tablespoon coconut oil
- 2 whole beaten eggs

Directions:

1. Take your 3-Quart Instant Pot; open the top lid. Plug it and turn it on.
2. In the cooking pot area, add the ingredients. Using a spatula, stir the ingredients.
3. Close the top lid and seal its valve.
4. Press "RICE" setting. It will automatically set cooking time.
5. After the set cooking time ends, press "CANCEL" and then press "NPR (Natural Pressure Release)".
6. Instant Pot will slowly and naturally release the pressure.
7. Open the top lid, add the cooked recipe mix in serving plates.
8. Serve and enjoy!

Nutritional Values (Per Serving):

Calories – 412

Fat – 11.5g

Carbohydrates – 42g

Fiber – 3g

Protein – 5.5g

Pure Pear Berry Cakes

Prep Time: 10-15 min.

Cooking Time: 35 min.

Number of Servings: 2-3

Ingredients:

- 1/4 teaspoon baking soda
- 1/4 teaspoon cardamom, ground
- 4 tablespoons milk
- 1 cup flour
- 3 tablespoons maple syrup
- 1 tablespoon flax seeds
- 4 tablespoons cranberries, chopped
- 1 1/2 cup water
- 1/4 teaspoon baking powder
- 1 tablespoon vegetable oil
- 1/2 cup pear, cored and chopped

Directions:

1. In a bowl, mix the baking soda, flour, cardamom, milk, flax seeds, baking powder, maple syrup and oil and stir well.
2. Add the chopped pear and cranberries, stir. Add the mix into a greased cake pan.
3. Pour the water and place steamer basket/trivet inside the pot; arrange the pan over the basket/trivet.
4. Close the top lid and seal its valve.
5. Press "MANUAL" setting. Adjust cooking time to 35 minutes.
6. Allow the recipe to cook for the set cooking time.
7. After the set cooking time ends, press "CANCEL" and then press "QPR (Quick Pressure Release)".
8. Instant Pot will quickly release the pressure.
9. Open the top lid, add the cooked recipe mix in serving plates.
10. Serve and enjoy!

Nutritional Values (Per Serving):

Calories - 286

Fat – 12g

Carbohydrates – 34.5g

Fiber – 9g

Protein – 5g

Conclusion

Instant Pot is a recent modern cooking invention that cooks food in one pot in real quick time. Instant Pot preserves nutrients in the food and provides you with healthy meals every day. A 3-Quart Instant Pot model is a perfect kitchen partner to make meals seamlessly without spending much time on cooking.

We sincerely hope that the book has succeeded in its aim to educate the readers about preparing wholesome Instant Pot recipes for small servings. We ascertain that the versatile methods covered in the book will help all its readers to transform their everyday diet and lead a quality lifestyle.

As always, cooking is an interpretation, so be creative and add your own touch to these recipes to make your customized version and share with your whole family.

Thank you and have a great time enjoying the delicious recipes!

Best of luck in all your endeavors! Happy Cooking!

80476302R00062

Made in the USA
San Bernardino, CA
28 June 2018